Just For Today
8 weeks

www.gratitudeandmore.ca

This journal was created with the intention of helping those in recovery with their daily inventory. It is by no means a complete checklist, but my hope is that it will assist with spot check inventories taken at any time of the day.

Each day has two pages, one with daily prompts and one lined page for any additional writing. There is also a Weekly Check-In page that allows you to review the previous week and set your intention for the coming days.

The purpose of the daily questions is to allow you to reach deep into yourself and discover the place where the answers are—but usually remain hidden. Only those brave enough to begin the excavation will reap the rewards.

Finally, the back pages are there for you to fill in any new contact information. I hope you enjoy your journey over the next eight weeks.

For more information on the wide variety of journals we offer, visit us at www.gratitudeandmore.ca

I wish you luck on your journey. Stay open.

Leah

WEEKLY CHECK-IN

My Intention for Next Week:

I would like to:

Experience...

Let go of...

Feel...

Learn to...

Stop...

I want more of...	I want less of...

Date:	Mood/Happiness Scale (1-10):
	AM PM

I am grateful for:

What is happening in my life today?

Was I of service?	Did I share how I was feeling?
I'm excited about:	Did I enrich my spiritual life?
What am I fearful of?	Do I owe an amend?
Did I struggle today?	Why?
Was I kind?	My plan for tomorrow:
Was I Hungry, Angry, Lonely or Tired?	

I am comfortable in my body and all is well.

| Date: | Mood/Happiness Scale (1-10): |
| | AM PM |

I am grateful for:

What is happening in my life today?

Was I of service?	Did I share how I was feeling?
I'm excited about:	Did I enrich my spiritual life?
What am I fearful of?	Do I owe an amend?
Did I struggle today?	Why?
Was I kind?	My plan for tomorrow:
Was I Hungry, Angry, Lonely or Tired?	

_____

_____

_____

_____

_____

_____

_____

_____

_____

_____

_____

_____

_____

_____

_____

_____

_____

_____

_____

Ruach: An explosive, expansive, surprising, creative energy that surges through all things. (Ancient Hebrew)

Date:	Mood/Happiness Scale (1-10): AM PM
I am grateful for:	
What is happening in my life today?	
Was I of service?	Did I share how I was feeling?
I'm excited about:	Did I enrich my spiritual life?
What am I fearful of?	Do I owe an amend?
Did I struggle today?	Why?
Was I kind?	My plan for tomorrow:
Was I Hungry, Angry, Lonely or Tired?	

To thine own self be true. (William Shakespeare)

Date:	Mood/Happiness Scale (1-10): AM PM

I am grateful for:

What is happening in my life today?

Was I of service?	Did I share how I was feeling?
I'm excited about:	Did I enrich my spiritual life?
What am I fearful of?	Do I owe an amend?
Did I struggle today?	Why?
Was I kind?	My plan for tomorrow:
Was I Hungry, Angry, Lonely or Tired?	

Dare to be remarkable!

Date:	Mood/Happiness Scale (1-10): AM PM
I am grateful for:	
What is happening in my life today?	

Was I of service?	Did I share how I was feeling?
I'm excited about:	Did I enrich my spiritual life?
What am I fearful of?	Do I owe an amend?
Did I struggle today?	Why?
Was I kind?	My plan for tomorrow:
Was I Hungry, Angry, Lonely or Tired?	

Abundance flows through me. I am a channel for the Universe.

Date:	Mood/Happiness Scale (1-10):
	AM PM

I am grateful for:

What is happening in my life today?

Was I of service?	Did I share how I was feeling?
I'm excited about:	Did I enrich my spiritual life?
What am I fearful of?	Do I owe an amend?
Did I struggle today?	Why?
Was I kind?	My plan for tomorrow:
Was I Hungry, Angry, Lonely or Tired?	

Rise! Do not shrink.

Date:	Mood/Happiness Scale (1-10): AM PM

I am grateful for:

What is happening in my life today?

Was I of service?	Did I share how I was feeling?
I'm excited about:	Did I enrich my spiritual life?
What am I fearful of?	Do I owe an amend?
Did I struggle today?	Why?
Was I kind?	My plan for tomorrow:
Was I Hungry, Angry, Lonely or Tired?	

You are worthy. You are important. You are loved.

REVIEW OF LAST WEEK

How balanced was my time? (work/family/Me)	Did I get outside every day for fresh air?
Did I have the support I needed?	Did I ask for help when I needed it?

Did I remember my intentions from last week?

Did I spend enough time being unplugged?

I am proud that I....

Notes:

WEEKLY CHECK-IN

My Intention for Next Week:

I would like to:

Experience...

Let go of...

Feel...

Learn to...

Stop...

I want more of...	I want less of...

Date:	Mood/Happiness Scale (1-10): AM PM

I am grateful for:

What is happening in my life today?

Was I of service?	Did I share how I was feeling?
I'm excited about:	Did I enrich my spiritual life?
What am I fearful of?	Do I owe an amend?

Did I struggle today?	Why?

Was I kind?	My plan for tomorrow:
Was I Hungry, Angry, Lonely or Tired?	

The Universe is conspiring with you, never against you.

Date:	Mood/Happiness Scale (1-10): AM PM

I am grateful for:

What is happening in my life today?

Was I of service?	Did I share how I was feeling?
I'm excited about:	Did I enrich my spiritual life?
What am I fearful of?	Do I owe an amend?
Did I struggle today?	Why?
Was I kind?	My plan for tomorrow:
Was I Hungry, Angry, Lonely or Tired?	

All that I seek is already within me.

Date:	Mood/Happiness Scale (1-10): AM PM

I am grateful for:

What is happening in my life today?

Was I of service?	Did I share how I was feeling?
I'm excited about:	Did I enrich my spiritual life?
What am I fearful of?	Do I owe an amend?
Did I struggle today?	Why?
Was I kind?	My plan for tomorrow:
Was I Hungry, Angry, Lonely or Tired?	

I am guided by my intention. I am open to the Universe.

Date:	Mood/Happiness Scale (1-10): AM PM
I am grateful for:	
What is happening in my life today?	
Was I of service?	Did I share how I was feeling?
I'm excited about:	Did I enrich my spiritual life?
What am I fearful of?	Do I owe an amend?
Did I struggle today?	Why?
Was I kind?	My plan for tomorrow:
Was I Hungry, Angry, Lonely or Tired?	

I am unlimited. My life is filled with abundance.

Date:	Mood/Happiness Scale (1-10):
	AM PM

I am grateful for:

What is happening in my life today?

Was I of service?	Did I share how I was feeling?
I'm excited about:	Did I enrich my spiritual life?
What am I fearful of?	Do I owe an amend?
Did I struggle today?	Why?
Was I kind?	My plan for tomorrow:
Was I Hungry, Angry, Lonely or Tired?	

I have freed myself from fear and self-doubt.

Date:	Mood/Happiness Scale (1-10): AM PM

I am grateful for:

What is happening in my life today?

Was I of service?	Did I share how I was feeling?
I'm excited about:	Did I enrich my spiritual life?
What am I fearful of?	Do I owe an amend?
Did I struggle today?	Why?
Was I kind?	My plan for tomorrow:
Was I Hungry, Angry, Lonely or Tired?	

I am in sync. I flow with the river of life.

Date:	Mood/Happiness Scale (1-10): AM PM

I am grateful for:

What is happening in my life today?

Was I of service?	Did I share how I was feeling?
I'm excited about:	Did I enrich my spiritual life?
What am I fearful of?	Do I owe an amend?
Did I struggle today?	Why?
Was I kind?	My plan for tomorrow:
Was I Hungry, Angry, Lonely or Tired?	

I choose to release fear, anger, hurt and resentment.

REVIEW OF LAST WEEK

How balanced was my time? (work/family/Me)	Did I get outside every day for fresh air?
Did I have the support I needed?	Did I ask for help when I needed it?

Did I remember my intentions from last week?

Did I spend enough time being unplugged?

I am proud that I....

Notes:

WEEKLY CHECK-IN

My Intention for Next Week:

I would like to:

Experience...

Let go of...

Feel...

Learn to...

Stop...

I want more of...	I want less of...

Date:	Mood/Happiness Scale (1-10): AM PM

I am grateful for:

What is happening in my life today?

Was I of service?	Did I share how I was feeling?
I'm excited about:	Did I enrich my spiritual life?
What am I fearful of?	Do I owe an amend?
Did I struggle today?	Why?
Was I kind?	My plan for tomorrow:
Was I Hungry, Angry, Lonely or Tired?	

I forgive others; I love myself and deserve the freedom it brings.

Date:	Mood/Happiness Scale (1-10):
	AM PM

I am grateful for:

What is happening in my life today?

Was I of service?	Did I share how I was feeling?
I'm excited about:	Did I enrich my spiritual life?
What am I fearful of?	Do I owe an amend?
Did I struggle today?	Why?
Was I kind?	My plan for tomorrow:
Was I Hungry, Angry, Lonely or Tired?	

How do you act authentically?

Date:	Mood/Happiness Scale (1-10):
	AM PM

I am grateful for:

What is happening in my life today?

Was I of service?	Did I share how I was feeling?
I'm excited about:	Did I enrich my spiritual life?
What am I fearful of?	Do I owe an amend?
Did I struggle today?	Why?
Was I kind?	My plan for tomorrow:
Was I Hungry, Angry, Lonely or Tired?	

I am open to new experiences and new people.

Date:	Mood/Happiness Scale (1-10): AM PM

I am grateful for:

What is happening in my life today?

Was I of service?	Did I share how I was feeling?
I'm excited about:	Did I enrich my spiritual life?
What am I fearful of?	Do I owe an amend?
Did I struggle today?	Why?
Was I kind?	My plan for tomorrow:
Was I Hungry, Angry, Lonely or Tired?	

Be still and know that I am God. (Psalm 46:10)

Date:	Mood/Happiness Scale (1-10): AM PM

I am grateful for:

What is happening in my life today?

Was I of service?	Did I share how I was feeling?
I'm excited about:	Did I enrich my spiritual life?
What am I fearful of?	Do I owe an amend?
Did I struggle today?	Why?
Was I kind?	My plan for tomorrow:
Was I Hungry, Angry, Lonely or Tired?	

I am patient, tolerant and filled with compassion.

| Date: | Mood/Happiness Scale (1-10): |
| | AM   PM |

I am grateful for:

What is happening in my life today?

Was I of service?	Did I share how I was feeling?
I'm excited about:	Did I enrich my spiritual life?
What am I fearful of?	Do I owe an amend?
Did I struggle today?	Why?
Was I kind?	My plan for tomorrow:
Was I Hungry, Angry, Lonely or Tired?	

I love every cell of my beautiful self.

Date:	Mood/Happiness Scale (1-10): AM PM

I am grateful for:

What is happening in my life today?

Was I of service?	Did I share how I was feeling?
I'm excited about:	Did I enrich my spiritual life?
What am I fearful of?	Do I owe an amend?
Did I struggle today?	Why?
Was I kind?	My plan for tomorrow:
Was I Hungry, Angry, Lonely or Tired?	

I am protected and safe.

REVIEW OF LAST WEEK

How balanced was my time? (work/family/Me)	Did I get outside every day for fresh air?
Did I have the support I needed?	Did I ask for help when I needed it?

Did I remember my intentions from last week?

Did I spend enough time being unplugged?

I am proud that I....

Notes:

WEEKLY CHECK-IN

My Intention for Next Week:

I would like to:

Experience...

Let go of...

Feel...

Learn to...

Stop...

I want more of...	I want less of...

Date:	Mood/Happiness Scale (1-10):
	AM PM

I am grateful for:

What is happening in my life today?

Was I of service?	Did I share how I was feeling?
I'm excited about:	Did I enrich my spiritual life?
What am I fearful of?	Do I owe an amend?
Did I struggle today?	Why?
Was I kind?	My plan for tomorrow:
Was I Hungry, Angry, Lonely or Tired?	

My body is strong and supports me in all I do.

Date:	Mood/Happiness Scale (1-10):
	AM PM

I am grateful for:

What is happening in my life today?

Was I of service?	Did I share how I was feeling?
I'm excited about:	**Did I enrich my spiritual life?**
What am I fearful of?	**Do I owe an amend?**
Did I struggle today?	**Why?**
Was I kind?	**My plan for tomorrow:**
Was I Hungry, Angry, Lonely or Tired?	

My life is unfolding with ease.

Date:	Mood/Happiness Scale (1-10): AM PM

I am grateful for:

What is happening in my life today?

Was I of service?	Did I share how I was feeling?
I'm excited about:	Did I enrich my spiritual life?
What am I fearful of?	Do I owe an amend?
Did I struggle today?	Why?
Was I kind?	My plan for tomorrow:
Was I Hungry, Angry, Lonely or Tired?	

My days are filled with excitement and love.

Date:	Mood/Happiness Scale (1-10): AM PM

I am grateful for:

What is happening in my life today?

Was I of service?	Did I share how I was feeling?
I'm excited about:	Did I enrich my spiritual life?
What am I fearful of?	Do I owe an amend?
Did I struggle today?	Why?
Was I kind?	My plan for tomorrow:
Was I Hungry, Angry, Lonely or Tired?	

Serenity is not the absence of conflict, but the ability to cope with it.

| Date: | Mood/Happiness Scale (1-10): |
| | AM   PM |

I am grateful for:

What is happening in my life today?

Was I of service?	Did I share how I was feeling?
I'm excited about:	Did I enrich my spiritual life?
What am I fearful of?	Do I owe an amend?
Did I struggle today?	Why?
Was I kind?	My plan for tomorrow:
Was I Hungry, Angry, Lonely or Tired?	

At the center of your being you have the answer; you know who you are and you know what you want. (Lao Tzu)

Date:	Mood/Happiness Scale (1-10):
	AM PM

I am grateful for:

What is happening in my life today?

Was I of service?	Did I share how I was feeling?
I'm excited about:	Did I enrich my spiritual life?
What am I fearful of?	Do I owe an amend?

Did I struggle today?	Why?

Was I kind?	My plan for tomorrow:
Was I Hungry, Angry, Lonely or Tired?	

Everyone has a story. It's not how you tell it. It's how you live it.

Date:	Mood/Happiness Scale (1-10): AM PM

I am grateful for:

What is happening in my life today?

Was I of service?	Did I share how I was feeling?
I'm excited about:	Did I enrich my spiritual life?
What am I fearful of?	Do I owe an amend?
Did I struggle today?	Why?
Was I kind?	My plan for tomorrow:
Was I Hungry, Angry, Lonely or Tired?	

The two most important days in your life are the day you were born and the day you find out why. (Mark Twain)

REVIEW OF LAST WEEK

How balanced was my time? (work/family/Me)	Did I get outside every day for fresh air?
Did I have the support I needed?	Did I ask for help when I needed it?

Did I remember my intentions from last week?

Did I spend enough time being unplugged?

I am proud that I....

Notes:

WEEKLY CHECK-IN

My Intention for Next Week:

I would like to:

Experience...

Let go of...

Feel...

Learn to...

Stop...

I want more of...	I want less of...

Date:	Mood/Happiness Scale (1-10):
	AM PM

I am grateful for:

What is happening in my life today?

Was I of service?	Did I share how I was feeling?
I'm excited about:	Did I enrich my spiritual life?
What am I fearful of?	Do I owe an amend?
Did I struggle today?	Why?
Was I kind?	My plan for tomorrow:
Was I Hungry, Angry, Lonely or Tired?	

_____

_____

_____

_____

_____

_____

_____

_____

_____

_____

_____

_____

_____

_____

_____

_____

_____

_____

_____

The task ahead of us is never as great as the Power behind us.
(Ralph Waldo Emerson)

Date:	Mood/Happiness Scale (1-10):
	AM PM

I am grateful for:

What is happening in my life today?

Was I of service?	Did I share how I was feeling?
I'm excited about:	Did I enrich my spiritual life?
What am I fearful of?	Do I owe an amend?
Did I struggle today?	Why?
Was I kind?	My plan for tomorrow:
Was I Hungry, Angry, Lonely or Tired?	

It's all an inside job.

Date:	Mood/Happiness Scale (1-10): AM PM

I am grateful for:

What is happening in my life today?

Was I of service?	Did I share how I was feeling?
I'm excited about:	Did I enrich my spiritual life?
What am I fearful of?	Do I owe an amend?
Did I struggle today?	Why?
Was I kind?	My plan for tomorrow:
Was I Hungry, Angry, Lonely or Tired?	

Do you want to be right or do you want to be happy?

Date:	Mood/Happiness Scale (1-10): AM PM

I am grateful for:	

What is happening in my life today?	

Was I of service?	Did I share how I was feeling?
I'm excited about:	Did I enrich my spiritual life?
What am I fearful of?	Do I owe an amend?
Did I struggle today?	Why?
Was I kind?	My plan for tomorrow:
Was I Hungry, Angry, Lonely or Tired?	

*Each new day offers twenty-four hours of possibility and
moves you forward on your path.*

Date:	Mood/Happiness Scale (1-10): AM PM
I am grateful for:	
What is happening in my life today?	
Was I of service?	Did I share how I was feeling?
I'm excited about:	Did I enrich my spiritual life?
What am I fearful of?	Do I owe an amend?
Did I struggle today?	Why?
Was I kind?	My plan for tomorrow:
Was I Hungry, Angry, Lonely or Tired?	

Each day may not be good, but there is good in every day. (Alice Earle)

Date:	Mood/Happiness Scale (1-10): AM PM

I am grateful for:

What is happening in my life today?

Was I of service?	Did I share how I was feeling?
I'm excited about:	Did I enrich my spiritual life?
What am I fearful of?	Do I owe an amend?
Did I struggle today?	Why?
Was I kind?	My plan for tomorrow:
Was I Hungry, Angry, Lonely or Tired?	

The first step towards getting somewhere is to decide that you are not going to stay where you are.

Date:	Mood/Happiness Scale (1-10): AM PM
I am grateful for:	
What is happening in my life today?	
Was I of service?	Did I share how I was feeling?
I'm excited about:	Did I enrich my spiritual life?
What am I fearful of?	Do I owe an amend?
Did I struggle today?	Why?
Was I kind?	My plan for tomorrow:
Was I Hungry, Angry, Lonely or Tired?	

_It's not about being the best, it's about being better
than you were yesterday._

REVIEW OF LAST WEEK

How balanced was my time? (work/family/Me)	Did I get outside every day for fresh air?
Did I have the support I needed?	Did I ask for help when I needed it?

Did I remember my intentions from last week?

Did I spend enough time being unplugged?

I am proud that I....

Notes:

WEEKLY CHECK-IN

My Intention for Next Week:

I would like to:

Experience...

Let go of...

Feel...

Learn to...

Stop...

I want more of...	I want less of...

Date:	Mood/Happiness Scale (1-10):
	AM PM

I am grateful for:

What is happening in my life today?

Was I of service?	Did I share how I was feeling?
I'm excited about:	Did I enrich my spiritual life?
What am I fearful of?	Do I owe an amend?
Did I struggle today?	Why?
Was I kind?	My plan for tomorrow:
Was I Hungry, Angry, Lonely or Tired?	

The mind is slow in unlearning what it has been long in learning. (Seneca)

Date:	Mood/Happiness Scale (1-10):
	AM PM

I am grateful for:

What is happening in my life today?

Was I of service?	Did I share how I was feeling?
I'm excited about:	Did I enrich my spiritual life?
What am I fearful of?	Do I owe an amend?
Did I struggle today?	Why?
Was I kind?	My plan for tomorrow:
Was I Hungry, Angry, Lonely or Tired?	

Be ready at any moment to sacrifice what you are
for what you could become. (Charles Dubois)

Date:	Mood/Happiness Scale (1-10): AM PM
I am grateful for:	
What is happening in my life today?	

Was I of service?	Did I share how I was feeling?
I'm excited about:	Did I enrich my spiritual life?
What am I fearful of?	Do I owe an amend?
Did I struggle today?	Why?
Was I kind?	My plan for tomorrow:
Was I Hungry, Angry, Lonely or Tired?	

When one is willing and eager, the gods join in. (Aeschylus)

Date:	Mood/Happiness Scale (1-10):
	AM PM

I am grateful for:

What is happening in my life today?

Was I of service?	Did I share how I was feeling?
I'm excited about:	**Did I enrich my spiritual life?**
What am I fearful of?	**Do I owe an amend?**
Did I struggle today?	**Why?**
Was I kind?	**My plan for tomorrow:**
Was I Hungry, Angry, Lonely or Tired?	

_____

_____

_____

_____

_____

_____

_____

_____

_____

_____

_____

_____

_____

_____

_____

_____

_____

_____

_____

_____

_____

The real voyage of discovery consists not in seeing new landscapes,
but in having new eyes. (Marcel Proust)

Date:	Mood/Happiness Scale (1-10): AM PM
I am grateful for:	

What is happening in my life today?

Was I of service?	Did I share how I was feeling?
I'm excited about:	Did I enrich my spiritual life?
What am I fearful of?	Do I owe an amend?
Did I struggle today?	Why?
Was I kind?	My plan for tomorrow:
Was I Hungry, Angry, Lonely or Tired?	

There is no way to happiness. Happiness is the way. (Thich Nhat Hanh)

Date:	Mood/Happiness Scale (1-10): AM PM
I am grateful for:	
What is happening in my life today?	
Was I of service?	Did I share how I was feeling?
I'm excited about:	Did I enrich my spiritual life?
What am I fearful of?	Do I owe an amend?
Did I struggle today?	Why?
Was I kind?	My plan for tomorrow:
Was I Hungry, Angry, Lonely or Tired?	

Be the change you want to see in the world. (Mahatma Gandhi)

| Date: | Mood/Happiness Scale (1-10): |
| | AM   PM |

| I am grateful for: |

| |

| |

| |

| What is happening in my life today? |

| |

| Was I of service? | Did I share how I was feeling? |

| I'm excited about: | Did I enrich my spiritual life? |

| What am I fearful of? | Do I owe an amend? |

| Did I struggle today? | Why? |

| Was I kind? | My plan for tomorrow: |
| Was I Hungry, Angry, Lonely or Tired? | |

*If the only prayer you ever say in your whole life is "thank you",
that would suffice. (Meister Eckhart)*

REVIEW OF LAST WEEK

How balanced was my time? (work/family/Me)	Did I get outside every day for fresh air?
Did I have the support I needed?	Did I ask for help when I needed it?

Did I remember my intentions from last week?

Did I spend enough time being unplugged?

I am proud that I....

Notes:

WEEKLY CHECK-IN

My Intention for Next Week:

I would like to:

Experience...

Let go of...

Feel...

Learn to...

Stop...

I want more of...	I want less of...

Date:	Mood/Happiness Scale (1-10): AM PM
I am grateful for:	
What is happening in my life today?	
Was I of service?	Did I share how I was feeling?
I'm excited about:	Did I enrich my spiritual life?
What am I fearful of?	Do I owe an amend?
Did I struggle today?	Why?
Was I kind?	My plan for tomorrow:
Was I Hungry, Angry, Lonely or Tired?	

Believe in miracles, but do the footwork.

Date:	Mood/Happiness Scale (1-10): AM PM

I am grateful for:

What is happening in my life today?

Was I of service?	Did I share how I was feeling?
I'm excited about:	Did I enrich my spiritual life?
What am I fearful of?	Do I owe an amend?
Did I struggle today?	Why?
Was I kind?	My plan for tomorrow:
Was I Hungry, Angry, Lonely or Tired?	

Leave room—life's most treasured moments often come unannounced.

Date:	Mood/Happiness Scale (1-10): AM PM
I am grateful for:	

What is happening in my life today?

Was I of service?	Did I share how I was feeling?
I'm excited about:	Did I enrich my spiritual life?
What am I fearful of?	Do I owe an amend?

Did I struggle today?	Why?

Was I kind?	My plan for tomorrow:
Was I Hungry, Angry, Lonely or Tired?	

Be willing to accept a temporary inconvenience for a permanent improvement.

Date:	Mood/Happiness Scale (1-10): AM PM

I am grateful for:

What is happening in my life today?

Was I of service?	Did I share how I was feeling?
I'm excited about:	Did I enrich my spiritual life?
What am I fearful of?	Do I owe an amend?
Did I struggle today?	Why?
Was I kind?	My plan for tomorrow:
Was I Hungry, Angry, Lonely or Tired?	

Seek respect rather than popularity.

| Date: | Mood/Happiness Scale (1-10): |
| | AM   PM |

I am grateful for:

What is happening in my life today?

| Was I of service? | Did I share how I was feeling? |

| I'm excited about: | Did I enrich my spiritual life? |

| What am I fearful of? | Do I owe an amend? |

| Did I struggle today? | Why? |

| Was I kind? | My plan for tomorrow: |

| Was I Hungry, Angry, Lonely or Tired? | |

_____

_____

_____

_____

_____

_____

_____

_____

_____

_____

_____

_____

_____

_____

_____

_____

_____

_____

_____

_____

Is what you're doing today getting you closer to where you want to be tomorrow?

Date:	Mood/Happiness Scale (1-10):
	AM PM

I am grateful for:

What is happening in my life today?

Was I of service?	Did I share how I was feeling?
I'm excited about:	Did I enrich my spiritual life?
What am I fearful of?	Do I owe an amend?
Did I struggle today?	Why?
Was I kind?	My plan for tomorrow:
Was I Hungry, Angry, Lonely or Tired?	

Belief is simply acceptance without proof.

| Date: | Mood/Happiness Scale (1-10): |
| | AM   PM |

I am grateful for:

What is happening in my life today?

| Was I of service? | Did I share how I was feeling? |

| I'm excited about: | Did I enrich my spiritual life? |

| What am I fearful of? | Do I owe an amend? |

| Did I struggle today? | Why? |

| Was I kind? | My plan for tomorrow: |

Was I Hungry, Angry, Lonely or Tired?

The only people with whom you should try to get even with are those who
have helped you. (John E. Southard)

REVIEW OF LAST WEEK

How balanced was my time? (work/family/Me)	Did I get outside every day for fresh air?
Did I have the support I needed?	Did I ask for help when I needed it?

Did I remember my intentions from last week?

Did I spend enough time being unplugged?

I am proud that I....

Notes:

WEEKLY CHECK-IN

My Intention for Next Week:

I would like to:

Experience...

Let go of...

Feel...

Learn to...

Stop...

I want more of...	I want less of...

Date:	Mood/Happiness Scale (1-10): AM PM

I am grateful for:

What is happening in my life today?

Was I of service?	Did I share how I was feeling?
I'm excited about:	Did I enrich my spiritual life?
What am I fearful of?	Do I owe an amend?

Did I struggle today?	Why?

Was I kind?	My plan for tomorrow:
Was I Hungry, Angry, Lonely or Tired?	

Failure isn't being knocked down—it's staying down.

Date:	Mood/Happiness Scale (1-10): AM PM

I am grateful for:

What is happening in my life today?

Was I of service?	Did I share how I was feeling?
I'm excited about:	Did I enrich my spiritual life?
What am I fearful of?	Do I owe an amend?
Did I struggle today?	Why?
Was I kind?	My plan for tomorrow:
Was I Hungry, Angry, Lonely or Tired?	

What do you dream of when no one is watching?

| Date: | Mood/Happiness Scale (1-10): |
| | AM   PM |

I am grateful for:

What is happening in my life today?

Was I of service?	Did I share how I was feeling?
I'm excited about:	Did I enrich my spiritual life?
What am I fearful of?	Do I owe an amend?
Did I struggle today?	Why?
Was I kind?	My plan for tomorrow:
Was I Hungry, Angry, Lonely or Tired?	

The more we resist, the more stuck we become.

Date:	Mood/Happiness Scale (1-10): AM PM

I am grateful for:

What is happening in my life today?

Was I of service?	Did I share how I was feeling?
I'm excited about:	Did I enrich my spiritual life?
What am I fearful of?	Do I owe an amend?
Did I struggle today?	Why?
Was I kind?	My plan for tomorrow:
Was I Hungry, Angry, Lonely or Tired?	

Start each day with a sense of possibility.

Date:	Mood/Happiness Scale (1-10):
	AM PM

I am grateful for:

What is happening in my life today?

Was I of service?	Did I share how I was feeling?
I'm excited about:	Did I enrich my spiritual life?
What am I fearful of?	Do I owe an amend?
Did I struggle today?	Why?
Was I kind?	My plan for tomorrow:
Was I Hungry, Angry, Lonely or Tired?	

The same boiling water that softens the potato hardens the egg. It's about what you're made of, not the circumstances. (Unknown)

| Date: | Mood/Happiness Scale (1-10): |
| | AM   PM |

I am grateful for:

What is happening in my life today?

Was I of service?	Did I share how I was feeling?
I'm excited about:	Did I enrich my spiritual life?
What am I fearful of?	Do I owe an amend?
Did I struggle today?	Why?
Was I kind?	My plan for tomorrow:
Was I Hungry, Angry, Lonely or Tired?	

We know what we are but know not what we may be.
(William Shakespeare)

Date:	Mood/Happiness Scale (1-10): AM PM
I am grateful for:	
What is happening in my life today?	
Was I of service?	**Did I share how I was feeling?**
I'm excited about:	**Did I enrich my spiritual life?**
What am I fearful of?	**Do I owe an amend?**
Did I struggle today?	**Why?**
Was I kind?	**My plan for tomorrow:**
Was I Hungry, Angry, Lonely or Tired?	

I care not so much what I am to others as what I am to myself.
(Michel Eyquem de Montaigne)

REVIEW OF LAST WEEK

How balanced was my time? (work/family/Me)	Did I get outside every day for fresh air?
Did I have the support I needed?	Did I ask for help when I needed it?

Did I remember my intentions from last week?

Did I spend enough time being unplugged?

I am proud that I....

Notes:

New Contact Information

Contact Information:

Name: _____

Phone #: _____

e-mail: _____

Address: _____

_____

Birthday: _____

Met: _____

Name: _____

Phone #: _____

e-mail: _____

Address: _____

_____

Birthday: _____

Met: _____

Contact Information:

Name: _____

Phone #: _____

e-mail: _____

Address: _____

_____

Birthday: _____

Met: _____

Name: _____

Phone #: _____

e-mail: _____

Address: _____

_____

Birthday: _____

Met: _____

Contact Information:

Name: _____

Phone #: _____

e-mail: _____

Address: _____

_____

Birthday: _____

Met: _____

Name: _____

Phone #: _____

e-mail: _____

Address: _____

_____

Birthday: _____

Met: _____

Contact Information:

Name: _____

Phone #: _____

e-mail: _____

Address: _____

_____

Birthday: _____

Met: _____

Name: _____

Phone #: _____

e-mail: _____

Address: _____

_____

Birthday: _____

Met: _____

Contact Information:

Name: _____

Phone #: _____

e-mail: _____

Address: _____

_____

Birthday: _____

Met: _____

Name: _____

Phone #: _____

e-mail: _____

Address: _____

_____

Birthday: _____

Met: _____

Contact Information:

Name: _____

Phone #: _____

e-mail: _____

Address: _____

_____

Birthday: _____

Met: _____

Name: _____

Phone #: _____

e-mail: _____

Address: _____

_____

Birthday: _____

Met: _____

Contact Information:

Name: _____

Phone #: _____

e-mail: _____

Address: _____

_____

Birthday: _____

Met: _____

Name: _____

Phone #: _____

e-mail: _____

Address: _____

_____

Birthday: _____

Met: _____

Contact Information:

Name: _____

Phone #: _____

e-mail: _____

Address: _____

_____

Birthday: _____

Met: _____

Name: _____

Phone #: _____

e-mail: _____

Address: _____

_____

Birthday: _____

Met: _____

Contact Information:

Name: _____

Phone #: _____

e-mail: _____

Address: _____

_____

Birthday: _____

Met: _____

Name: _____

Phone #: _____

e-mail: _____

Address: _____

_____

Birthday: _____

Met: _____

Contact Information:

Name: _____

Phone #: _____

e-mail: _____

Address: _____

_____

Birthday: _____

Met: _____

Name: _____

Phone #: _____

e-mail: _____

Address: _____

_____

Birthday: _____

Met: _____

52477602R00087

Made in the USA
Charleston, SC
20 February 2016